Horatio Mortimer Loved Music

by

Sharon A. Harmon

Illustrated by

Siiri Paton

Sharon A. Harmon

First Edition September 2020

Title: Horatio Mortimer Loved Music

Author: Sharon A. Harmon

Illustrations and Cover Art: Siiri Paton

ISBN: 978-1-7354604-1-3

Published in cooperation with
Kane Publishing

Phillipston, Massachusetts

Dedicated to
FINN

Those who wish to sing always find a song.
~Plato

Horatio Mortimer loved music.
He looked for music all around him.

He traveled with
a big paper bag.

Horatio plucked a musical note from wind in the trees.

He pulled a musical note from
waves crashing to the shore.

He put them into his paper bag.

Then Horatio thought
there had to be more.

He captured a musical
note from the birds.

He grabbed a musical note
from a baby's laugh.

Then he pulled a note
from a poet's words.

He placed each lovely
note into his bag.

He found many musical notes
in the falling rain.

He got a hold of a musical note
from a big bullfrog.

He caught a musical note
from a whistling train.

Then added notes from a
barking dog.

Horatio didn't know how to
make the notes into music.

But then he had
a most musical idea.
Ah, ah!
He called his notes,
"The Song of the World."

Then Horatio traveled
with his notes to a man
who made music.

The music professor with
a large magic baton,

peered into
Horatio's big bag
of musical notes.

The professor said,
"I can make it into a song."
Then he waved his magical wand.

"Open it!" The professor cried.
A shiny string of colorful notes flew
out of the bag and into the sky.

Music poured through the air,
lovely tunes flew everywhere.
Horatio smiled.

**Horatio Mortimer
loved music.**

CPSIA information can be obtained
at www.ICGtesting.com
Printed in the USA
BVHW020026191020
591302BV00002B/7